Irish Tinkers

D0786596

Photographed and compiled
with a foreword and transcr
Martina O'Fearadhaigh

St. Martin's Press
New York

Copyright © 1976 by
Janine Wiedel, Martina O'Fearadhaigh

All rights reserved. For information, write:
St. Martin's Press, Inc., 175 Fifth Ave.,
New York, N.Y. 10010

Library of Congress Catalog Card Number:
76-62799
First published in the United States of
America in 1978

ISBN 0 312 43627 0

Printed in the U.S.A.

Dedication

to the Tinkers
of Ireland

The authors and publishers would like to make it quite clear
that the transcripts alongside the photographs are not the words
spoken by the people depicted in that particular photograph.
However each quotation is an accurate transcription of the words
of Irish tinkers interviewed by the authors

Foreword

Origins

The origins of Irish tinkers have been the subject of numerous theories and much controversy for some time. Irish tinkers themselves readily identify with any number of theories of origin as the occasion suits :

Well it happened in Scotland during the Clearances, it happened in Ireland with Cromwell. We are born into times of persecution when countrymen were dividing the lands. That's what has us blackguarded that we don't know our names rightly and the right way of saying what happened to the lands and all belonging to us....

9

Modern scholars have suggested that tinkers are descendants of the dispossessed from such times of social and economic upheaval as Cromwell's infamous 'to Hell or to Connaught' campaign, the Battle of the Boyne (1690), the Battle of Aughrim (1691) and the Irish potato famines of the nineteenth century. Many earlier writers suggested theories as to the origin in the British Isles of tinkers and of *shelta*, their secret language.[1] MacAlister (1937)[2] has received much notice for his discovery of 'one of the lost languages of the world' and MacNeill (1919)[3] proposed one of the most original theories, namely that tinkers had been members of an early Celtic population of rivet-makers known in Irish as *Tuath Semon*.[4] MacNeill believed that this caste had an important social function as menders of weapons for warriors, but were later relegated to inferior status by the invading Gaels. As well as providing historical explanation for the link between tinkers and the craft of metal-working, MacNeill's theory also suggests a background for the prejudice of settled folk towards tinkers. Other more 'creative' theories infer that the tinkers are vestiges of 'reparees' or free-booters[5] who roamed the countryside and were makers of counterfeit coins ; or that they were members of criminal bands who took refuge in *clauchauns* (bee-hived shaped dwellings) ;[6] or are descended from the ancient Picts[7] or other Celtic peoples.

The 'displaced lord' theory[8] is particularly attractive to Irish tinkers because it gives them a strong sense of identity linked with the land. According to this view, the tinkers were originally attached to lords as vassals or in some minor capacity, and followed the feudal custom whereby servants of the nobility bore the family name. Even today, some tinkers claim that they still wander in traditional feudal 'cuts' that have been unlawfully wrested from them and they frequently call themselves 'knights of the road'. The fact that until recently

notes p 13

Irish tinkers elected 'kings' at horse fairs in rural parishes helped to perpetuate the image of 'tarnished nobility' : although, in fact, 'a king had no more authority by virtue of his title than he would...have because of his position as the senior male parent of his immediate family.'[9]

It is clear from this conglomeration of speculation and folklore that few things are certain about the origins of Irish tinkers. They should not be confused with Gypsies or Romanies, who are thought to hail from India, and speak Romany, a language of Sanskrit origin. The arrival of tinkers in Britain almost certainly pre-dates that of Gypsies in the twelfth or thirteenth century. It may also be possible that the tinkers of Wales, Ireland and Scotland originated independently of one another although they do have some characteristics in common. Today, with increased mobility, all these groups have mixed to some degree and, outside of Ireland, the tinkers have mixed with Gypsies[10] which clouds the issue further. Some Irish tinker families live in Atlanta, Georgia;[11] and some others may have emigrated to Australia, and countries such as Sweden[12] and Holland[13] also claim indigenous tinker groups.

Definition

The word 'tinker' was derived from 'ceard' or 'tinceard'[14] and is an occupational definition. Whereas the term may have originally been a mark of prestige, today it generally has derogatory implications which in itself symbolises the occupational dysfunctionalism the tinkers now experience.

Until recently the official definition of the tinker in Ireland was that he was someone :
who had no fixed abode and habitually wandered from place to place, but excluding show people and travelling entertainers...[15]
In England the Gypsy has been similarly defined :
persons of nomadic way of life, whatever their race or origin but does not include members of an organised group of travelling showmen...[16]
Because of the possible pejorative context of the word 'tinker', the Irish government termed tinkers 'itinerants'. This reflects the long-standing predilection of tinkers for the word 'traveller', in itself a means of evading the occupational dysfunctionalism and a way of emphasising what the tinkers are most proud of – their travelling aspect.

Whilst I respect the wishes of the tinkers to be called 'travellers', in this foreword I have used the old word solely because both Gypsies and tinkers are calling themselves 'travellers' and I wished to make a clear distinction between the two.

Occupation and Stratification

Tinkers are members of a subcultural minority group[17] in which membership is established by claiming that one or both parents are tinkers; and by a certain ability to speak shelta although this is not a decisive factor. While officials are engaged in defining various types of Gypsies, tinkers and half-bloods, tinkers themselves have their own way of distinguishing between 'them' and 'us'. If a tinker marries into a Romany tribe it is said, 'He married worse than a tinker.' If a tinker marries a settled person (called buffer, countryman, quality, or gentry) he will probably no longer be recognised as a tinker.

In response to industrialization & urbanisation, many tinkers have given up their traditional crafts such as tinsmithing, flower-making and spoon-mending, and have taken up scrap-dealing. This development is facilitated by the increasing use of motor lorries rather than horse-drawn bow-topped caravans,[18] and motorised caravans rather than 'bow', 'bender' or 'humpie' tents.[19] When the 'Economic Classification of Itinerant Families'[20] was compiled it was noted that there were three main groupings : the motor-trailer group of 40-60 families who were the affluent dealers ; the horse dealers who still used the horse-drawn caravan comprising 300-400 families and a third group of 350-450 families who had horse-drawn caravans or tents. Only the third group retained the tinsmithing affiliation and this kept them in a poorer income range.

With the introduction of plastic and industrial technology which made tinsmithing a less lucrative trade, the tinkers adapted themselves to scrap-dealing. Status within the group now depends on the ability to amass large amounts of wealth in terms of horses, caravans, motor lorries and scrap. The major scrap-dealers 'lend' such goods to the poorer ranks of tinker society thus fulfilling an economic need. Each class within the subculture has its own particular dialect of shelta which identifies the tinker as a member of that class. The only way out of this strictly defined order is to 'pass' into the settled way of life which in itself is an arduous task.

Absorption, Integration, Passing

A great dilemma faces Irish tinkers today as it does tinkers everywhere and Gypsies must experience similar pressures. The refinement of municipal byelaws, tarmacing of roads and encroaching urban development force the tinkers to adapt to the modern world. Scrap-dealing, forced on the tinkers when their traditional crafts became redundant, sets them apart from their neighbours not least because of the eyesore caused by their scrap heaps. Nevertheless their attitudes to settlement and education remain ambivalent. To some the possession of a house and good schooling are means of gaining entry into the settled community. To others these 'yokes' (things) are encumbrances. To some extent, it appears that tinkers value survival by one's wits, the inner wisdom that comes from cruel experiences of the life on the road and respect for the family more highly than the possession of a set of educationally derived conventions existing outside their cultural context.

A policy of absorption might well fail to reach all Irish tinkers partly, as we have seen, as a result of the highly stratified nature of the subculture. Membership is fluid and many families may be said to be between subcultures or on the verge of passing into settled society. The disintegration of old family ties perhaps marks the end of the old way of life but the tinkers have in the past proved themselves to be extraordinarily adaptable to new situations. Perhaps, just as many tinkers are able to pass in one or more traveller groups, they will also master the technique of passing for 'tinkers' or 'settled' folk as the occasion demands.

> We are all very conscious…that the process of integrating itinerants is killing off a very fine and a very valuable subculture in our lives…Itinerants on the roads have a great deal to contribute to the Irish national life.
>
> We must find that and try to preserve what was in it.[21]

Martina O'Fearadhaigh

1 *see:*
   C G Leland
   The English Gypsies and their Language
   London, 1873
   C G Leland, 'Shelta'
   Gypsy Lore Society Journal
   (New Series, vol I, 1907)
   D MacRitchie, 'Shelta: the Cairds Language'
   Transactions of the Gaelic Society of Inverness
   vol 24, 1901
   K Meyer, 'The Secret Languages of Ireland'
   Gypsy Lore Society Journal
   (New Series, vol II, 1909)
   J Sampson, 'Tinkers and their Talk'
   Gypsy Lore Society Journal
   (Old Series, vol II, 1891)
   J Sampson
   The Dialect of the Gypsies of Wales
   Oxford University Press, 1926,
   reprinted 1968
   W Simson
   A History of the Gypsies
   London, 1865
2 R A Stewart MacAlister
   The Secret Languages of Ireland
   Cambridge University Press, 1937
3 E MacNeill
   Phases of Irish History
   Dublin, 1919
4 Ibid
   p75, suggests that the group was
   also known as *Semonrige* or *Semaine*
5 Unsigned article
   The Sphere
   December 1956, pp462–63: 'An Irish Tinker
   on the Road.'
6 Jean Paul Clébert
   The Gypsies,
   translated by Charles Duff, Penguin,
   London, 1967
   pp85–86 (quoting Murray) describes a fanciful
   exploration in which several authors compare
   Gypsies with a description of fairies whose
   'dwellings had the form of bee-hives made of
   stones or interlaced willow rods or turf.
   It seems that, in the first fine days of their
   existence, the fairy people left their house
   and spent the whole summer in the open air.'
7 MacNeill, op cit, p75

8 Electra Bachman O'Toole, 'An Analysis of
   the Travelling People of Ireland'
   Gypsy Lore Journal
   Third series vol XIX, pp60–61, 1973
9 Report of the Commission on Itinerancy
   Dublin, August 1963, p38
10 Christopher Reiss
   Education of Travelling Children
   Macmillan, London, 1975, p53
11 Jon Nordheimer, 'Colony of Nomadic Irish
   Catholics Clings to a Strange Life in the South'
   New York Times
   14 October 1970, p49
12 A Heymowski
   Swedish Travellers and their Ancestry
   Almqvist and Wiksell, Uppsala, 1969
   Also see Reiss, op cit.
13 Reiss, op cit
14 Sampson (1891), op cit
15 Report of the Commission
   op cit, pp12-13
16 Caravan Sites and Control of Development Act
   1968, part II
17 For further discussion of tinker society see
   Farnham Rehfisch, 'Marriage and the
   Elementary Family among the Scottish Tinkers'
   Scottish Studies
   vol V, part 2, 1961
18 C H Ward Jackson and Denis E Harvey
   The English Gypsy Caravan
   David & Charles, 1972, p84
19 *Scotland's Travelling People*
   Scottish Development Department
   Edinburgh, 1971, p37
20 The Stationery Office
   Dublin, 3 August, 1963, pp79–83
21 Dr Birch, 'Itinerants Have Much to Offer'
   The Kilkenny People
   30 October 1970, p6

13

Irish Tinkers

Tinker camps may differ in detail but the first impressions are always
the same : the sounds of barking dogs and neighing horses mingle
with the smells of boiled cabbage and wood smoke as they filter
through the air from the camps of squat canvas tents and wooden
caravans. An assortment of multi-coloured laundry hangs from trees
and across stone walls, waiting for a few moments of Irish sunshine.
A swarm of muddy children gather round, some with hands out-
stretched, others lingering in the background, all watching intently.
Along the dirt track women appear at doorways and from beneath
tent flaps and gaze with silent suspicion at the intruder.

Makeshift dwellings bear witness to the itinerant nature of the
tinkers' existence but beneath this 'gipsy' cliche displayed to the outside world I discovered a people whose way of life became of com-
pelling interest to me. Each year since 1970 I have returned to Ireland
to visit and photograph the tinkers. Through the combination of
their words and my photographs I hope to show something of this
world which captivated me. It is a way of life based on extraordinarily close family ties by which relatives living great distances
from each other, and without the facilities of reading and writing,
still know how the other members are and ardently protect the
family name. There is a resistance to the acquisition of material posses-
sions, born of the practical limitations of space when stationary & of
encumbrance when mobile ; an honest philosophy of making do,
using other people's spare change - trees as washing lines, a farmer's
field for grazing their ponies, scrap tin for making pots and pans.
Children are taught to live by their wits ; accepting death and trouble
with the same fatalism as they would storms and bad weather ; and,
above all, tinkers have an ability to survive independently and, remain-
ing, until recently, unfettered by the persuasions of education,
television and the authorities to conform.

I would like to thank those tinkers who appear in the photographs
in this book as well as the many families who also shared their hospi-
tality with me & whose photographs I have not been able to include.

Over the years there have been many hours of sorting words
and printing photographs and without the friendship, advice and
encouragement of Michael Kaufmann and Peter Rea the project
might never have progressed. I am therefore specially pleased that
Peter Rea has designed this book.

Janine Wiedel

Well, it happened in Scotland and it happened in Ireland.
You get tinkers everywhere. That's the bother of being born in
times of prosecution when people are uprooted from their homes
and forced on the side of the road. We're being moved on every day
and they're tarmacing the road so you just remember the old times....

19

20   Like I have a sister and she can do queer pulls of things and
      no one can explain it. One night she was putting up the clothes
      on the thorn tree when she heard the sound of a grave crying in
      her ear. And when she heard it she knew her baby was dead,
      it was its little ghosteen. And when she went into the tent
      the fate was on it in it. The baby had fallen into the fire and was
      killed that minute.
      Like, with all that sorrow and grieving, you can't be surprised
      when it happens. You can't be gone out of your head when you see
      a bad storm coming or anything because that's the way it happens
      with us....

      Some travellers have four or five lives. There is a man named
      John. I found him choking to death with the smoke of the caravan.
      One day, tea cooking in the pot ready for him, I found him drowned
      in the river and breathing water and he ran into a man's trailer
      and he beat him silly with a stick. Another day he was punched up
      so bad he was concussed we thought for life and he's been in and
      out of death but he's a devil for living and there's no one can
      put him down completely....

She wasn't allowed for to pick us up to hold us & we were standing around her. At a fair she got a weakness come on her one time, it was the Tramore Races. And a crowd of people stood packed like animals round her. She was fainted. You'd think one of the horses had died. It was no great funeral. She got up and we hanging on her skirts because she could never pick us up in her arms on account of her weakness. One time the bus driver wouldn't let her on a bus. He'd a thought there was a fight. But there wasn't. Mammy's nose was bleeding like a river. Me daddy said he'd make tins free of charge for the bus driver to take his tea in so then he let them on despite the bleeding that was going on all over the place....

There are no more tinkers, Daughter, no more. If there was,
you'd have to go and make a spleen over it. Some say we took to
the road with a curse that hung over us since Cromwell. Some say
we're the old families from before the Famine and we have the old
family names of the old Celtic lords. But there's no more tinkers.
Not since the time of the Black Stranger and ever since we're
eating out our history on the old dole money....

'My little son,' I said. 'My little son you are not well !'
'Mother,' he says, 'Mother, I can't see the sugar ! Do I go out
to the stream for it? I can't see it.' I said, 'Can you hear your
mother with her black eye talking to you, son? Do you hear
your mother that's talking to her own first-born?' And he says,
'Mother, don't be daft but I can't see the sun and it looks like
it's snowing everywhere.' 'Son,' I says to him, 'have you been
after drinking in the ways of your wicked and tormented father
whose half way inside his grave at the age of forty-two?' 'No,'
he says, and he raking his hair with a little mousey-coloured comb.
I thought someone had surely put the curse of Moses on him
& he was not quite right in his head that is for definite certain....

Irish Tinkers

I'd like to be inside a house myself but I'm not ready. The townspeople has a list & I think it goes by the number of children you have.
If you have ten children then you gets a house quicker than if you have
three like me. If you talk nice and low to them when they come and
the children say hello and shake the hand and have a nice red ribbon
in the hair they take a respect on that family and that family is
going to get a house first....

When you're on the road, the children help to put up the tent,
feed the animals, & they wander around & soon before you know it,
three dead. They fell into the blackest water ever put between you
me and God. There's no way out of children. You're supposed to
have them. Half the time I was wishing they'd be gone when they'd
be gone - out chasing hares or after some wild thing....

Mine go to school.
  Many Mammies don't want their children in school.
      Oh they make out to the settled folk they do
                because it's
the very good and best thing you could say to that kind of person.
You got a house quicker you know if you say things rightly. Well,
I send mine to schools because I want them no ways on the road
like me, like I almost got off it for good. They learn how to be
spoiled in school. The big one he fights crazy with the others,
but the little one, she's got very lady-like altogether, sitting down
in a corner playing quiet like. I love them when they come home
so pleased. When I come home I always brings them sweets and
they always grab a milk bottle and drinks it down the whole thing.
I couldn't teach them manners the way school does do the job for me....

I see no harm in it letting the children do for themselves with
a little bit of education, but, if it's all the same to you, they
gets a fair amount of that at home with all they have to do–
shouting for the horses in the morning and calling for their dogs
in the field and they do knows how to tie a rope to more than a
little dog, and how to skin a cat ; they knows how to catch a fish
in the river with a piece of grass, how to throw a whistling sound
to the colt, a whistling coat to the foxes and how to take a chicken
from the jaws of a stoat, & 'tis no mean education they gets out of
the hammering of tin and the hammering of their mother's voice
on their little animal ears....

Schools can fix children in a bad way you know. It's better you'd
keep them out of it betimes. Some of them treats their children
terrible. They don't give what they want in the line of nourishment
or contentment....

Irish Tinkers

The garda was going to put them in a school up in the mountains
where they do be digging turf for their dinner and walk in their
feet naked in the snow like sheep and goats. A boy got taken up
for begging & he was sent at six to such a place out in the wilderness.
He got leave for the holidays. You could hear him crying
this couple of mile over : Mammy, don't send me back. They feed us
nothing but the worms that are pricking the tomatoes, & the work
we do be getting would break a cow better than yoke a bull.
 And the poor mother was heart-scalded over the tragedy that had
befallen the child....

36

If you ask : What's the time? do you have the time?, people do
be vexed and they stare at you with their calculations as if
you were riding about in a painted dream on the old horse & cart.
We have black teeth but we dream just the same as the people that
live in houses. Just to be born on the side of the road is to go down
in disrespect. I know a man went down in Australia and he came back
in Ireland as a tinker but they still had no respect for him....

I know verses by heart and my Mammy taught them to be my songs. In the town they used to ask me : how did you get to sing like that? I used to say oh er I picked them up. You see I didn't like for them to be knowing I sang to the babies to make them bonny when they got big and I didn't like for them to hear the class of songs I knew. But those songs can make me cry and it's no book that wants my tears....

Saint Paul chased the snakes out of Malta but he did not chase
me out of this bogland so look around sharp in my eye. You would
laugh to see the mud come in my door but it still does be coming in.
My poor baby has thrush and I'll look around for Dr Fever coming
down the road. He's coming with a little shovel of ashes for my baby.
May God increase the length and breadth of your wisdom for having
seen a real traveller in an apron speak to you in the weak light
of the Famine's morning....

When I was small and went for water up
the ditch where my Mammy sent me
I saw the houses, standing up high over
the hills and trees, some of them.
I often thought betimes to meself I wonder why
we're sitting outside waiting for to go inside.
Mammy brought me inside houses with her
when she went every Thursday. Sometimes
they'd sprinkle holy water on us and sometimes they'd harm us with a few hard knocks
and curse us passing....

The Lone Ranger never saw the ways my Daddy drinks and Mammy
lets the bawling out of her when she sees him. Wasn't that a queer
time when we used to watch them coming home drunk when we was
but small wee children barely out of the stork's mouth. We used to
make fun of them & play games about the way they were. But you
know drunk people is no different from the rest of us. Drunk is all the
time the only way to be if it's winter and you haven't a blanket for a
child or let a drop of milk fall into his mouth first before you go out.
Mammy never forgot us though she'd always bring us a crust or
something for us, sweets, when she came back. I'm not saying evil
against her or any ill fit for Hell or Heaven because she never did us
no wrong. The drink on them makes travellers and other poor folk
cry and bawl and I'm only afraid for the neighbours as we like to
keep that kind of practice right within the family. In town they all gets
drink on them and they all carry on in the pub until it's past the closing
and then they come falling down the road and get caught out
in the frost....

I just combed her hair and said there now child go off and play
and I patted her head with the sides of the comb to make her fine.
I always plaited her hair that time in the morning and then she
went out playing somewhere, I don't know where ; & that morning
they found the where, in the long plaited grasses by the river
where she was drowned, may God rest her soul, and I never saw
the place before because we never went swimming, until we went
swimming that day for to get her little body out and I had a pot
of stew hanging on the fire waiting ready hot for to give her.
I threw it out on the grass rather than give it my dead,
my dear, dead, daughter. My young son came running in and he says
to me, 'She's stuck, she's stuck, God help her!' He was so young
he didn't know what had happened. He didn't know she was dead.
Oh, my poor dear dead daughter, may God rest her! I hurled myself
at her grave. I wrecked myself. I drank myself. I threw white paint
and ashes at me mouth. I didn't want to live after and I swore
I'd have no more children after. But I got ten children now,
God bless them all, but it's not the same as my Bridget,
may God rest her!

Irish Tinkers

For a woman a house is a grand thing for her to put the children in.
But for a man a house is only a payment of rents. I knew a travelling family there in some town and they never pays rent and they'll
be put out one of the days. Lots of travellers have houses in the
winter and they leaves them lonely when they take to the roads
in the summer. It's only a bother having the house and it's not
healthy to be shut inside them four walls with no trees in sight
and only the windys to keep you half breathing. No, I'd sleep in a
stables before I'd sleep in a house....

61

I never think about being a traveller or getting a house 'cause
those people when they settle you they just think of getting rid
of you, and they don't care where they put you. What we want
is a nice clean decent house like our caravan...I've talked to
many people and they all have answers to the problem, and I listen
to the wireless and I know more about it than they do. They're getting nicer to travellers but they're forgetting a few things.
I don't like the old days. I like what's going now. But they're
not giving us a fair chance to think what we are and who we are.
They think we're all the same, like we were cattle or some kind
of circus animal that's roaming wild....

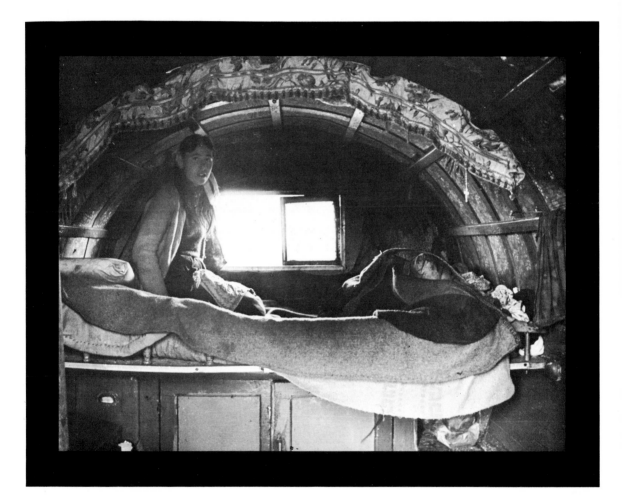

We're queer ways travelling people. One night we'll stay and one night we'll not and we'll have the whole camp gone up and thrown into a cart, cocks and roosters and goats and all the crockery and the kettle bar and all your belongings heaped together in a heap on the back of the cart....

66

68

The black smile that is hanging from your mouth does be making me
afraid to talk about it – my childhood and what went wrong – but
I fell out with my life on the road as soon as I was borned into it.
Is it I could put a stone between my eyes to find the day my son
died at three months old. I could beat some sense into the mares
that lick the mizzen stars on their first born foals. I could choke with
tears when I think of the queer little sagging bones of my son, my poor
dear dead son, my poor little dead son, ageing in his grave this year....

I don't interfere with the wife and children.
          If they wants to go begging I wouldn't stop them, but I minds my business
                    & don't interfere too much with the country people unless it's my own way of doing
                              the business with them. You won't see men travellers begging.
                         It's 'cause of their pride. In the old days the men did all the begging
                      and they broke stones for their bread, helped out in the fields and all.
                         Well, today you won't see that...To my mind I wouldn't beg
                      'cause they'd only tell you to work and you couldn't answer them
              like a poor woman with a baby under her shawl. The women bring in
                 good money begging and betimes I'd see them with great suits for
                    me and the children so I'd pay them no heed for begging.
                                        It's no sin,

is it?

Some other women betimes calls me in for tea in a cafe and I feel
like a black. I just can't go in because my sister-in-law is begging
with the baby dropping pennies on the floor of the establish-
ment. How could I go in when my own flesh and blood is begging
and that's my son she has borrowed for the day?

We are the rag and bone. We are the summer walkers of the long
acre of widow Breen. We are the men of the rag and bone and we've
come to pick the potato eyes out of the quality folk. We are knights
of the road. Some do call us that and we've come to comb the gristle
out of the meat of the country men. They are not the real gentry
you know. There's a flaw in them that takes one wife, leaves go
of her go and then takes on another and what will you have for
your tea tomorrow sir?

There was a man who had an Alsatian, finer than any whippet
for catching hares. If he could get his teeth under your jumper
he would and betimes he very nearly did. You'd have your boots
torn out from under you, your knees black with cold, your coat torn
off from your back. He had strong teeth this dog and he was a good
watch dog too. On the road you need some kind of canny dog.
This dog he could stare anybody down. He had green eyes, handsome
green eyes like a snake you might say. You might say he was be-
witched or an enchanted dog but to my ways of thinking he was just
very ordinary like, you know, very ordinary & he knew his business
and his reason for staying on the road to protect the travellers....

These two friends Willie and Joseph were spitting at each other
with the talk that came out of them. They had a few drinks on them
and the moon was hidden in their pockets – you couldn't see it.
They were going home with the old horse and cart but both of them
were so tired out with the drink they were laying lazy on the back
of the cart. They kept beating the donkey. They beat the donkey
till their hands bled. Then they see a green light. (Now you know
Jack O'Lantern ; if he was born 2000 years ago he'd be dead long ago
but as it is he was born in recent times. He will stay till the world
comes to an end so he will.) He is green and sometimes red
but this night he was green. Willie and Joseph when they did see
this green light they didn't know what to do. They beat the poor
animal more and more till at last stones were in their breath
& they were fagged out altogether. They came closer to this green
light then and seen it was a garda. 'I'm a garda', he said,
'I'm a policeman', and he let go of a stick on their heads and the
two let out a wailing would frighten the saints up in Heaven.
'And the light is green', he said, 'and I'm going for to make out
a warrant & summons for speeding & cruelty to this poor animal.'

There could be a dozen wives up the road that is beat near to death.
It's a very old thing. You can get burnt ten times a day and you
can get beat near to death more often than that and nobody won't
say nothing. The women do sport their black eyes in the town and
people will know how they got it and they do stride very proud of
what they got like but I wouldn't think that kind of thing was a
thing to be flashing the tackles about. You can hear some kind of
argumentation going on in the next tent and you daren't come
out & let on 'cause that might lead to ructions within the families
and that might go on for weeks till everybody is knocked flat
and it will never stop. So it is the custom that if you hear something going on and you know what it is you make out that you
don't know what it is. The women bite the cloth so their neighbours don't hear them screaming. Well, they don't spend half
their life in labour laughing. You just put up with it like you do
the frost & the strong winters that we do be having in these parts....

84   The reason I don't want to knit is because I might become a nun
     and go simple and wear them eyeglasses...That's why I go out and
     buy my baby rich hats of blue and pink to make people laugh.
     When I was young I made baskets. I made baskets then, yes I did.
     Everybody said I had the tendency and flair for to make baskets
     so I continued to make them. Everyone was fairly satisfied with
     the results. But I do need them glasses to restore the alphabet.
     To write I need double thick glasses and then I couldn't see my baby.
     My poor baby, oh my poor dear father. Can you see him, child,
     through the smoke? Can you see your uncle in Scotland. He fell
     off a scaffold and he has his poor arm in a sling. Now all his
     brothers are going to fetch up the body with his arm in a sling
     for the funeral.
     People try and make out that travellers take things, that anything
     a rough child's hand passes over it disappears, It isn't so.
     I'd like to stand up and tell people different. That night on
     the hay my body was bruised black and blue like the blackthorn
     tree and still my baby is born a traveller and there is nothing
     I can do. Birds are flying upside down in this world and there's
     nothing that can put a straight man on a crooked road but speech
     this side of earth.
     My uncle was the greatest knitter Heaven sent us. It is true he
     could knit a cardigan the length of this road into town and back.
     Here comes my husband. Can you tell he's my boyfriend? Yes my
     very own husband? Does he have the look on him that he is mine?
     Well, I'll give him two black eyes for leaving me here starving
     with ten children. Well, soon he'll have the look on him that he is
     my husband....

You know you can't go to the cinema with your husband even after
you marry him. A married woman won't speak to her husband if
they happen to meet in town by chance. She won't even nod to him.
That shows him decent respect, do you understand?

We'd never go into a house 'cause there would be neighbours.
We don't agree with that. What kind of life would I have if I had
gone in with me family - no peace and boozing and God knows what.
If I was in a house 'twould be the same thing. People from the
town visiting me. Neighbours bringing me warm milk for the starving
children when my wife feeds them well. People bringing blankets
and all when we have them. We're travellers - our children are -
so what the use of pretending we're wanting charity handfuls,
when we're better off providing the little bit we're needing-
we live better than rich people....

Now England is a place you can buy lots of swag, plastic elephants, plastic gnomes, plastic foxes, plastic lambs. I can pick up the thread of my life in Scotland in the tattie fields. In Africa you hear they are starving from them whose hands make a business of charity and they say, they say in Biafra they are starving! Well, I'm starving here beside the two red hot coals of a fire I have my mind on and I don't need no Biafra to tell me a grain of rice would put sense in China and feed us for a week. And in Africa, I've heard tell they have the blacks all herded together and whip them to make them work. I knows what it's like to be a black and to have the spit of nine men on your tail. Yes, I've been all over and I know well the life in Scotland, Ireland and that's what it is and there it is, that's where I've been at all at all–

I'll have you know their father is a fit and proper tinsmith too. His father's tongue is on him. He comes of decent stock. He knows the look of money shining from the metal side. He knows the talk of money too at fairs when fairs is called and he can laugh at a good picture and flash the tackles for the men if that's what they're asking for in the way of punches and the lot. There isn't a thing that he lacks. He can argue with a stone & bring the tears from your eyes. He can solder a brand on a hare when your back is turned agin him, or put a horseshoe on the moon....

I used to get me horses for the work I'd do. I'd like a horse
now and again 'cause I could swap him in a fair and no one would
know the difference if he brought back his old horse twice in
the same fortnight. I could fix them good as new and put an old
bottom coat right back in that horse - cover up his weak spots in his
teeth, I used to do so he looked a right smart lively and good-
looking animal. In payment I used to gets me soup, tea and horses
and sometimes even a cat or dog. Depends what I'd take me fancy to.
I used to do a lot of work on credit. I'd be in the habit of clean-
ing yards and then when I'd earned me all of it I'd git the use
of a field or the use of a meadow and the horses too. No tres-
passing going on in those days 'cause all the fields were ours
and we got our share of the beet & turnip too. Whatever there was
we got our fair share....

92

Plastic is what put us out and that's in it all. Because plastic
is what we use today. Nobody wants aluminium today save for a
few shops and out the country. But people laugh at tinsmithing today and selling the tins harder than collecting scrap today.
Nobody rightly wants tin in their houses. Everyone says you can
make a fine living on tin, but today won't tin maybe buy you a hand-
shake with a priest and that's all....

I'm not a tinsmith but I can makes me anything in tin from a
frying pan and to a teapot and a spokes. I can make me a stakes,
a tea drawer, anything. It's running in my blood and you can tell
by the cut of me I'm a tinsmith. Daddy was too....

This is how I makes a cup if yer want to know how's the thing done.
I sits with the anvil like a saddle between me legs. I just pick up
my hammer or a stick that says to me it is going to make a right
hammer, and I just hit the tin plate just straight between
the eyes that's looking back at me in the mirror of me soul, and
I just put together the edges of the tin to make me a handle first,
and when I have the two edges bent straight in a line I hit the
shape into a ladle and leave it aside me. Then I take up me snips
and snip out the cup and with a clean tinwhistle you could see the
snips takin' all of the tin in. Then I cuts me the circle, the brim,
and I get me the rivets aside me, and I put it together with rivets
or I can solder in the fire if the fire is lazy and the solder is right.
It's the cleanest trade is the tin. But cleaner still is sweeping,
and you can clean the sky of sparrows with my little brushes....

Now when I get in a house I'll make me curtains and all and
tender little things for the kitchen. I'll paint the doors and windows
and cook a right fire on the hearthstone. But it won't be the same
as a camp & I'll miss all the fierce looking company around us now.
To tell you the truth, I wouldn't live in a house but I'd like to
have one all right to try it out and I could tell you after
what way I'd look inside the windows, with no gaffer on my back
and my face clean....

Irish Tinkers

Now I'm off the road I can speak about it plain. It's warm
and now when I walk down the street, if someone asks me for
to send me a letter I can tell me I have me own address and all
and they can read it out to me & know where to come to visit me.
I like the country for the summer. The fresh air and sun and
the riding through the countryside, you'd meet very fair looking
people in the country, not the same as in town places. I'd be lonely
after the road. I like being settled. But I like the road and there's
no use telling you a lie when you're putting for to speak to me....

They want something from us. We want something from them.
We want the houses and the education. We got the Catechism and
we got Confession & we got the Marriage Certificates & we got
dole money. They've got our horses put away from us & they've got
our cuts fenced with little gates. That's the way they wanted it.
Now we want education so we can read and write but it don't
mean that we're not travellers. They can't take away the blood
that's rolling around in our veins now, can they, not when you have
a drink taken & remember your name handed on for generations....

Irish Tinkers

I've been to Scotland. I've been to Spain. I've been every
country in the world and if I'd the chance again I'd do it again.

That was before I met my wife and had a bit of travel left in me....

I can make tin buckets, about twenty in a day. Copper is harder
to work in, and that would take me three days to do the same.
I know designs that was handed down these generations, & one day
a tourist stopped me and she took pictures of my work but she never
came back…It's dying out, the trade. It's fit for tourists and that.
In a few years, I think it will be gone. In the old days everyone
needed some tin gallons for the tea for the workers but it's all
changed now. My father was in the town in the old days. Like in
the fairs he'd set himself down, and people would come to him
begging for him to mend the tins & things. Now this doesn't happen.
I have to go out to the big shops and ask is there anything fit going.
If they'd feel like it, they'd say yes. In the old days the people was
a lot more good-natured and mannerly. It's the new crowd got
the money now and goes to dances. They don't buy tins no more
and have electric cookers and that, and you can see your television has
everyone talking like fancy actors….

True as God, I can do any sort of work at all. I can dig ditches,
mend rails, hammer plates, & saucepans, lead horses, doctor animals.
I can tarmac, sing, dance, fiddle, & play a tune on the tin whistle.
I can harvest, turn a plate of rashers, lid the saucepan, and fiddle
with a motor, build a car, mend a shaft and sell any trinket.
I am a tool-maker as well – the only one in the district. The rest
is scattered through the hills 'cause the English drove them out –
they were so bad looking with their snips ready to snip them out of
Ireland. I've reared me children on the road ; was born, raised
and reared and bred on the road myself ; and I was making churns,
buckets, gallons, anything you'd ask for. But don't ask now as
I'm not able for it. To tell you the truth, I was never at a wake
where they didn't drink from one of my cups and one of my candles
didn't burn at the bedside of the corpse….

We don't read and we don't write. What we do is sing. That
is the way out of the tragedy of the life on the road, and it does be
a lonely life at that. Diddling and crying is the only way out,
to tell you it can make you friendly with yourself....

We used to gather for a wedding. There was one a while back there.
The bride wore white. Sixteen families came from Wales, twenty
from England, two from the Isle of Man, fifty from around Galway &
Mayo. And we went into a pub and had a right old time and no one to
disturb us. Even the guards were drinking that day. Then we went into
the car park and some fiddlers came up and we had the whole town
dancing for three days. That's what you get with big families.
There was the sight of drink you've never seen - a hundred cases
gone every minute, and the old man supplying the lot on account of
his being the godfather. The townspeople put on ribbons for us
that time and they invited our children to play with theirs.
It wasn't like we were tinkers at all. You'd think you were at a funeral
there was never such respect shown to the living before us....

When someone dies, a drink is the only way to forgive that person for going so lonely on us and leaving us in the ways of understanding about him that he's gone and left someone to mourn after. And a laugh is as good at a time like that and a story to make all the family happy again so they can take their grief out to bed with them and forgets all about it until sunrise and then the drink will take it all out of them so they'll forget who died....

The travellers will burn a caravan where a dead person has been. They don't believe in keeping it on like. They don't believe in letting ghosts about the place and so they burn everything. They bury the travellers in the poor old paupers graveyard, betimes with his best rig out, betimes without a harness or bridle. But it is said that it's right and a decent and fitting thing for a travellers' caravan to be burned. Some goes again' it & they have the likes of ghosts moving about and messing about the tent and I wouldn't put up with that now, would you?

The families are all getting settled now and that's the end of
the fairs, the fights & the lot of it. It's the same way there are
no more smiths, carpenters, no more dealers except in lorries....

If I could change my life I'd ask that I had a house but could
leave it and pay no mind. I'd ask that I had my family by my side.
I ask for a bite to eat and no more....

I know an old couple round of seventy years. Ten years in a house
they were. When they see'd death was to come on them in a house,
they took to the roads, sold the house and everything for two fine
white horses. That's the way with the travellers. I've travelled
England and every part of Ireland. You can't leave all that for
one little house with shutters to shut you up quarrelling, and
a chimney to clean every day and wife to cook on the old hearth.
I spend half my days in houses working so I see all I wants of them then....

Betimes it do be peaceful on the road.
I get a queer feeling when I do hear the goats
scratching on the bark of the trees and they
hop around in the branches and they rock
the caravan of an evening & I lean out & tell them
get off heifer, get off rooster, get off, get off,
and don't be rocking the old caravan.
The wind does have the best job in doing that.
There's no need for you to scratch me ears out
with your midnight goings on.